The Craft of Smocking

By the same authors
Quilting in Squares

COVER PICTURES

The Craft
of Smocking

Katharine Fisher & Elizabeth Kay

Diagrams by Katharine Fisher

Photographs by Joseph Berger

Charles Scribner's Sons   New York

Copyright © 1979 Katharine Fisher and Elizabeth Kay

Library of Congress Cataloging in Publication Data

Fisher, Katharine.
  The craft of smocking.

  Includes index.
  1. Smocking. I. Kay, Elizabeth, joint author.
II. Title.
TT840.F56   746.4′4   78-27335
  ISBN 0-684-16082-X

1 3 5 7 9 11 13 15 17 19 Q/P 20 18 16 14 12 10 8 6 4 2

Printed in the United States of America

To Stuart, who finally admitted "Deary" could write books, and to Walt, who always knew we could!

ACKNOWLEDGMENTS

We wish to thank our students and especially Debby Russell and Mimi McMennamin, the very first, for getting us started; Kit, Lowrie, and Connie Fisher, who modeled the grown-up clothes; and Sarah Fisher, who insisted on smocked blouses for her bridesmaids; Jim Kay for wearing the fancy dress shirt; Mary Lamb Harding for lending us Becky's pinafore; Lynn and David Kay for all the preliminary picture taking; and Jan Moller for her help.

We would also like to recommend to you Grace L. Knott's book *English Smocking* (Ontario: G. Lyons).

CONTENTS

# INTRODUCTION

The art of smocking is one of the few peasant handicrafts of England that has been carried on for hundreds of years. English smocking is decorative embroidery worked over gathered pleats. American smocking is different because the pleats and embroidery are gathered and worked at the same time. This makes it difficult to finish with the correct size, a problem that often discourages people from trying to smock.

English smocking has a ratio. For every inch of finished smocking you should allow approximately 2½ inches of material. This gives the necessary elasticity for a good fit and makes it easy to adapt commercial patterns for smocking.

Smocking is not as hard as it looks. It is both creative and satisfying. The embroidery stitches are very much the same as in crewel work or needlepoint, but are more like crewel in the way they are "freely" sewn over the material. Smocking can be as artistic as needlepoint and crewel and all other forms of embroidery.

Smocking is smashing! It is not just the little girl's dress you remember from your childhood. You can enhance your wardrobe with creative smocking on nightgowns, blouses, sundresses, and even on a fancy dress shirt front for the man in your life.

Getting Started

MATERIALS

Today's materials are perfect for smocking because smocking is never ironed. Use lightweight Dacron and cotton blends, calicos, soft flannelette, or challis. They are wash-and-wear. Don't use corduroy, denim, velvet, or any heavy material because they will not gather into the proper pleats.

Plain color or printed material may be used, but if you are a beginner, start with the plain; you'll see the stitches more clearly.

You will need embroidery thread for working the smocking stitches and an embroidery needle with a long, thin eye. You'll also need a spool of dark regular sewing thread and a regular needle for "picking up the dots."

There are two types of dots, which come in sheets, evenly spaced. They come in yellow or blue. One may be transferred to the material with an iron; the other type is sewn onto the material and leaves no stamp marks. The sew-on dots are good for dark printed material, where it is next to impossible to see the stamped-on dots. Sheets of dots must be ordered by mail because at the present time they are unobtainable in stores. (See Chapter Four.)

Occasionally a commercial pattern includes a plain sheet of dots in the package. Dots are "picked up" with a needle and thread and form the guidelines for the smocking stitches. The threads are then gathered to make uniform pleats. The smocking stitches are worked on these pleats.

BE SMART—TO START
MAKE A SAMPLER OF STITCHES

Sampler I, Plate 1

Cut a piece of plain-color material 14″ long by 28″ wide. Be sure the selvages are at the sides (Fig. 1a).

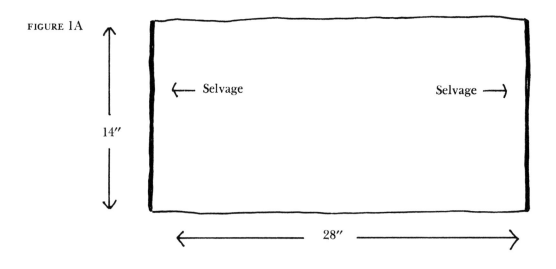

FIGURE 1A

14″

Selvage ← ← Selvage →

28″

Sampler I See front cover.

Cut off twenty-four rows of dots 25″ wide from a single sheet of blue transfer smocking dots. Place the material on the ironing board, *wrong* side up, with selvages at the sides. Center the strip of dots on the material, leaving a 2″ or 3″ border on each side—a few pins are helpful. Use a moderately hot iron and iron from one side across the dots to the other. Peek to see if the dots appear. If all is well remove the paper and throw it away (Fig. 1b).

FIGURE 1B

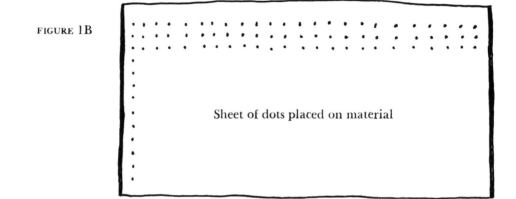

Sheet of dots placed on material

PICK UP TIME

Diagrams are drawn for right-handed people; lefties simply reverse them.

This is the one time you'll need a long, long piece of thread in the needle—the length of the dot row. Start with the second or third dot. Make a fat knot and go in one side of a dot and come out the other side of the *same* dot (Figs. 2a, 2b). Go on to the next dot and continue across the row, leaving two or three dots at the end. In a sampler it is helpful to see the dot rows. Do not knot the thread but leave a tail hanging. Careful—don't break the thread; the row must be sewn with one continuous piece and not gathered (Fig. 3). Three lines a day keeps the boredom away!

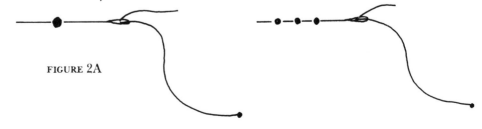

FIGURE 2A

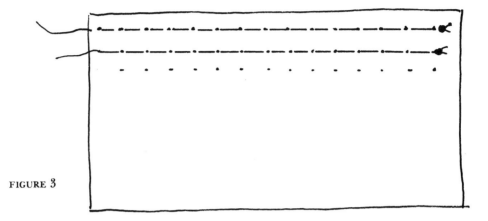

FIGURE 3

PULL UP TIME

All the dots have been picked up. You are ready to pull up the threads to make the pleats. Gather the first and second rows, at the same time pushing the fullness toward the knots. Now lay the sampler on the table and gently pull up each row one at a time. Helpful hint—keep the thread short and close to the sampler as you pull. This cuts down the chances of breaking the thread (Fig. 4). Adjust the pleats across the sampler so they

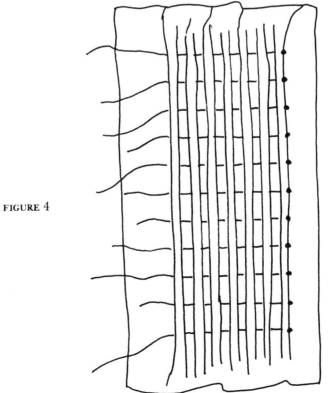

FIGURE 4

are even and uniformly spaced, close together but not jammed. Tie all the rows together in pairs. Cut the ends off but leave enough hanging so they can be untied if necessary. Turn the sampler over, pleats facing up.

FIGURE 5

• Top (dot row)	¾ way
¼ way	• bottom (dot row)
½ way	

THINGS YOU NEED TO KNOW

1. Stitches are made on the dot rows or in the spaces between the dot rows. The space between two dot rows may be divided into sections, as in Fig. 5. Stitches are taken on each pleat.
2. Smocking is done on the *right* side of the material.
3. Hold the sampler so that the pleats are horizontal and facing you, and the knots are nearest you and on the underside (Fig. 6).

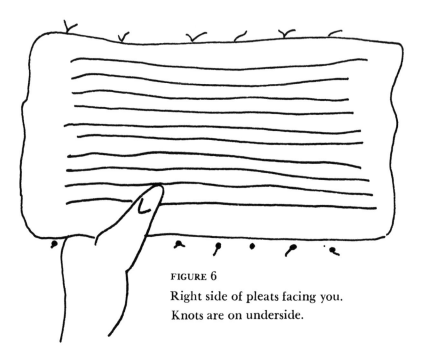

FIGURE 6

Right side of pleats facing you.
Knots are on underside.

GET READY TO START SMOCKING

Come up from underneath at the side of the first pleat about halfway between the top of the pleat and the dot row. The needle pierces the pleat and points directly at you. Pull through. Then go over to the second pleat, pierce it, and pull through to make the first stitch (Fig. 7). Start with the Outline stitch in Sampler I (the beginning sampler). This stitch is worked in a straight line across the row (Fig. 8).

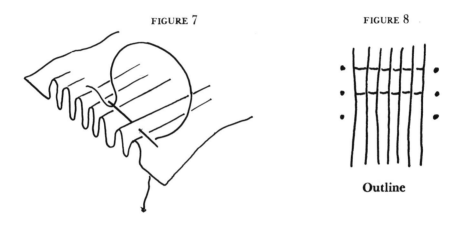

FIGURE 7

FIGURE 8

Outline

BEGINNING SAMPLER OF STITCHES

Outline   Fig. 8, rows 1 and 2 in Sampler I

Come up at the side of the first pleat.

1. Thread below the needle, go over to the second pleat, and take a stitch, keeping the needle level with the dot row.

2. Go to the next pleat and repeat; continue across the row, always keeping the thread below the needle.

   To end off: Go down to the underside exactly where the thread came out. Sew over and over on a pleat and snip the thread off.

   To begin again in the middle of a row: Come up exactly where you went down and start at the point where you left off.

Now let's learn the Cable stitch. This stitch is also worked in a straight line across the row (Fig. 9).

FIGURE 9

Cable

Cable   Fig. 9, row 3 in Sampler I

Come up at the side of the first pleat.

1. With the thread *below* the needle, go over to the second pleat and make a stitch, keeping the needle level with the dot row.
2. Now with the thread *above* the needle, go to the next pleat and make a stitch.

    Alternate the thread above and below the needle, working across the row and always keeping the needle level with the dot row.

The Baby Wave is the next stitch to learn. There is a very important rule to remember when moving up or down between the dot rows, or from one level to another.

Rule: Thread below the needle to go up. Thread above the needle to go down.

FIGURE 10

Start

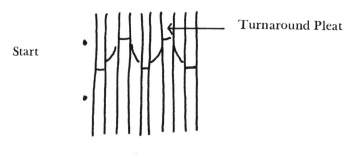

Turnaround Pleat

Baby Wave

Baby Wave   Fig. 10, row 4 in Sampler I

Sewn in space halfway between two dot rows.

Come up at the side of the first pleat.

1. With the thread *below* the needle go over to the next pleat and make a level stitch. (Remembering that a level stitch is a stitch that is made on the same level as the stitch just taken.)
2. Go to the next pleat up to the dot row and make a stitch (thread below).
3. With the thread *above* the needle go to the next pleat and make a stitch at the same level. This is the stitch that gets you set to go down. It is made on the pleat that we shall call the *turnaround pleat*.

8

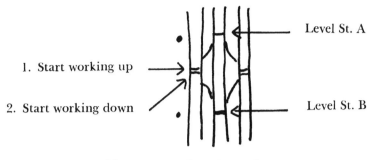

1. Start working up →

2. Start working down

Level St. A

Level St. B

FIGURE 11   **Baby Diamond**

Baby Diamond   Fig. 11, row 5 in Sampler I

Sewn in space between two dot rows.

    1. First make one row of Baby Wave, working up to the dot row.
    2. Make another row of Baby Wave, working down to the dot row.

Note: Level stitch A is in a direct line with and shares the same pleat as level stitch B. The pleat they share is the turnaround pleat, and it looks like one pleat.

You have learned the basic principles of smocking: how to stitch along a straight line and how to move up and down between the dot rows or on different levels. Let's go on and learn more creative stitches.

FIGURE 12

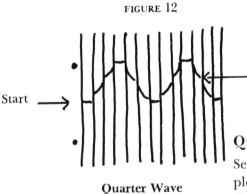

Start →

½

Quarter Wave

Quarter Wave   Fig. 12, row 6 in Sampler I

Sewn in space halfway between two dot rows, and using four pleats.

Come up at the side of the first pleat.

    1. With the thread *below* the needle go over to the next pleat and make a level stitch.
    2. Go over to the next pleat and make a stitch halfway up.
    3. Go over to the next pleat and make a stitch at the top.
    4. Now go to the next pleat and make a stitch at the same level but with the thread *above* the needle ready to go down (the turnaround pleat).
    5. Go to the next pleat at the halfway point.
    6. Go to the next pleat at the bottom.
    7. Go to the next pleat and make a level stitch with the thread *below* ready to go up.

9

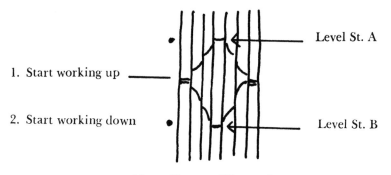

1. Start working up ———

2. Start working down

Level St. A

Level St. B

FIGURE 13   Quarter Diamond

Quarter Diamond   Fig. 13, row 7 in Sampler I

Sewn in space between two dot rows.

1. First make one row of Quarter Wave, working up to the dot row.
2. Make another row of Quarter Wave, working down to the dot row.

Note: **a.** Level stitch A is in direct line with and shares the same pleat as level stitch B.   **b.** There are four pleats contained inside the Quarter Diamond.

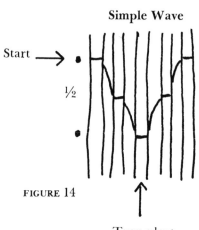

Simple Wave

Start ——→

½

FIGURE 14

Turn pleat

Simple Wave   Fig. 14, row 8 in Sampler I

Sewn in space between two dot rows.
Come up at the side of the first pleat.

1. With the thread *above* the needle go to the next pleat and make a level stitch.
2. Go to the next pleat and halfway down.
3. Go to the next pleat at the dot row.
4. Go on to the next pleat; make a level stitch with the thread *below* the needle, ready to go up. This is the turn-around pleat.
5. Go to the next pleat at halfway up.
6. Go to the next pleat at the dot row.
7. Go to the next pleat, with the thread *above* the needle, and make a level stitch on the *turn pleat*, ready to go down.

Simple Wave—Double   Row 9 in Sampler I

Make a Simple Wave. Follow along the wave, sewing on the same pleats either a little above *or* below the stitches.
It can be spaced close to the Simple Wave stitches or a half space away.

10

Large Wave   Fig. 15, row 10 in Sampler I

Sewn in space between two dot rows.

Come out at the side of the first pleat.

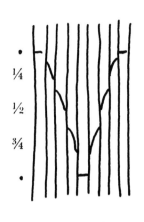

FIGURE 15

1. With the thread *above* the needle go over to the next pleat and make a level stitch, working down.
2. Go to the next pleat and make a stitch one-fourth of the way down.
3. Go to the next pleat and make a stitch halfway down.
4. Go to the next pleat and make a stitch three-fourths of the way down.
5. Go to the next pleat and make a stitch on the dot row.
6. Go to the next pleat (the turn pleat) and make a level stitch with the thread *below*, ready to go up.
7. Go up with the same spacing: one-fourth of the way, halfway, three-fourths of the way, and the dot row.
8. With the thread *above* the needle go over to the turn pleat and make a level stitch, ready to go down.

Large Wave—Double   Row 11 in Sampler I

Follow along the Large Wave, sewing on the same pleats either a little above *or* below the stitches.

It can be spaced close to the Large Wave stitches or a half space away.

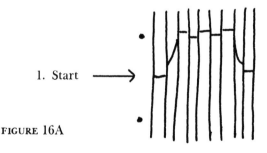

1. Start →

FIGURE 16A

Small Link   Figs. 16a and 16b, rows 12 and 13 in Sampler I

Row 12 is the top half of the Link and row 13 is the completed Link.

Come out at the side of the first pleat.

1. With the thread *below* the needle go to the next pleat and make a level stitch.

2. Go to the next pleat up to the dot row and make a level stitch.

3. Go on to the next pleat, and with the thread *above* make a level stitch. This is the first of five Cable stitches. Continue making four more Cable stitches, alternating the thread above and below the needle, running along the dot row. You are making a total of five Cables.

4. Now go to the next pleat at halfway down and make a stitch (thread *above*).

5. Go on to the next pleat (the turn pleat) and with the thread *below* make a level stitch, continuing across the row. This completes the top half of the Small Link.

6. Come out at the side of the first pleat just below and touching the first stitch in Fig. 16a.

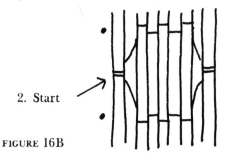

2. Start

FIGURE 16B

7. Go to the next pleat, with the thread *above*, and make a level stitch.

8. Go down to the dot row and make a stitch.

9. Go on to the next pleat and with the thread *below* make the first of five Cables. Continue making four more Cables, alternating the thread above and below the needle.

10. Go on to the next pleat at halfway up and make a level stitch with the thread *below*. This stitch is just under and touching the last stitch in Fig. 16a. Continue across the row. This completes the bottom half of the Small Link.

Large Link

This is worked the same as the Small Link but has seven Cables on the top and bottom instead of five.

Links may be any length but they should have an odd number of Cables. A variation: When starting, make three Cables instead of one level stitch.

12

2 COMBINING STITCHES

COMBINATIONS

FIRST COMBINATION   Baby Diamond Cable

Start halfway between two dot rows and come out at the side of the first pleat.

1. With the thread *below* the needle go to the next pleat and make a level stitch.
2. Then go up to the dot row and make three Cable stitches. You are now set to go down with the thread *above* the needle.
3. Go over to the next pleat at halfway down and make a level stitch (thread *below*). Continue across the row.
4. Make the lower half of the Baby Diamond Cable to correspond.

Be sure the stitches on the turn pleats are in direct line with one another and share the same pleats as in Fig. 11.

When making Cables, if you want to go up start the Cable with the thread *below* the needle. If you want to go down start the Cable with the thread *above* the needle.

SECOND COMBINATION   Turret

A good border stitch; worked between two dot rows. Make one row of Cable stitches on the top dot row. Make another row of Cable stitches on the bottom dot row.

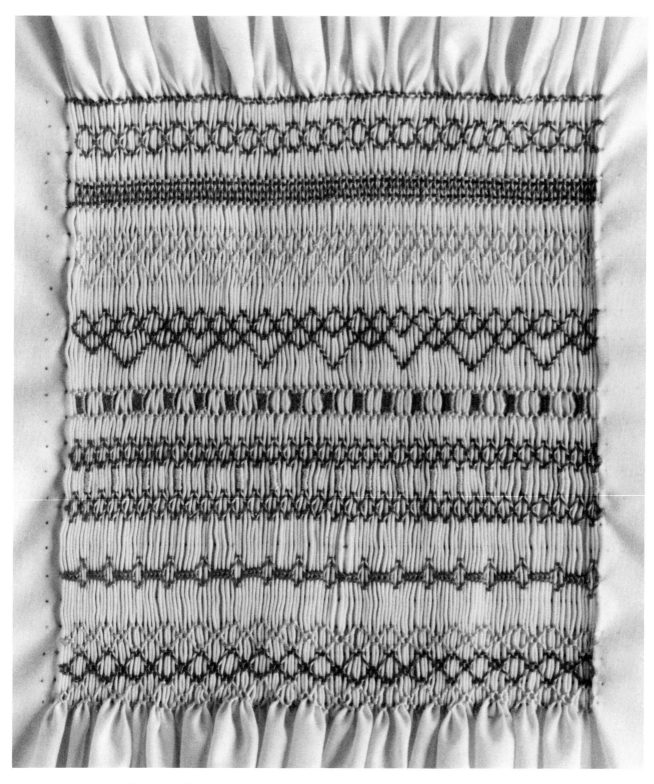

Sampler II See back cover.

1. Come out at the side of the first pleat on the bottom dot row just above the Cables. Go to next pleat and with the thread *below* the needle make a level stitch, ready to go up.
2. Go up on the *same* pleat to just below the top Cable, and make a stitch.
3. Go over to the next pleat and with the thread *above* make a level stitch ready to go down.
4. Go down on the *same* pleat and make a stitch on the bottom.
5. Move on to the next pleat with a level stitch, thread below ready to go up.

Turret can also be made without the Cable rows.

Rule in combining stitches: When making Waves, sometimes it is necessary to take more stitches on additional pleats in order to reach the turn pleat.

THIRD COMBINATION **Baby Diamond and Simple Wave**

Covers three dot rows.
1. Make the top row of Baby Diamonds.
2. Make the bottom row of Baby Diamonds. (Steps 1 and 2 are made between two dot rows.)
3. Start the Simple Wave by coming out at the side of the first Baby Diamond at the turn pleat.
4. Continue taking stitches on pleats until you reach the turn pleat that corresponds with the Baby Diamond turn pleat.
5. With the thread *below* the needle go up in the same manner.

FOURTH COMBINATION **Quarter Diamond Combined with a Quarter Diamond and Large Wave**

Covers three dot rows.
1. First row: a row of Quarter Diamonds.
2. Starting at the bottom of the first Diamond turn pleat, complete one Quarter Diamond.
3. Continue taking stitches on pleats for the Large Wave until you reach the turn pleat that corresponds with the above Quarter Wave pleat.

Spools between Cables

Covers two dot rows.

1. First make Cable stitches on the top and bottom dot rows.
2. To make Spools: Come up from the underside next to the Cable and catch four pleats together, sewing over and over. Go down to the underside, end off, and cut the thread. Start another Spool with a new piece of thread. Pull the thread firmly but not tightly.

SIXTH COMBINATION **Baby Diamonds and Bars**

Covers four rows.

1. Make a row of Baby Diamonds between row 1 and row 2, and another row between rows 3 and 4.
2. Connect the points with Bars. To make Bars: Come up from the underside and catch two pleats, sewing over and over. Then end off and start the next Bar with a new thread. (If bars in a design are close together you may carry the thread, but no more than three pleats.)

SEVENTH COMBINATION **Wheat Stitch**

Made of Outline and Baby Diamond; can also be made of Cable and Baby Diamond.

1. Make five Outline stitches with the thread *above* the needle on the dot row. (Your thread is automatically set to go up.)
2. Go halfway up the next pleat and make a stitch.
3. Go over to the next pleat (the turn pleat) and make a level stitch with the thread *above* the needle.
4. Then go down to the dot row; make a stitch, and then make five more Outline stitches with the thread *above* the needle. Continue sewing across the row, making Outline stitches and the top half of the Baby Diamond.
5. Make the bottom half: Come up at the side of the first pleat just below the first Outline stitch of the top row. With the thread *below* the needle make five Outline stitches.
6. Go halfway down and proceed along the row, making the bottom half of the Baby Diamond and Outline stitches.

Note that the two rows of Outline stitches, one made with the thread above the needle and the other with the thread below, give a herringbone effect.

EIGHTH COMBINATION **Cable Diamonds**

1. Start with the center row. Make three Cables. With the thread *below* the needle go up to the top and make three more Cables. With the thread *above* come down and make three more Cables. Continue across the row.
2. Add the bottom half of the Cable Diamond. Continue adding Cable Diamonds, making a series. Each row interlocks with the row above and below.

MORE STITCHES FOUND IN THE DESIGN SAMPLERS

FIGURE 17

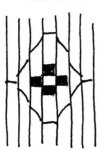

Flowerette

Flowerette   Designs 3 and 6 (page 20)

A good way to add a touch of color. It may be used in Diamonds that contain four or more pleats.

1. Make a Diamond.
2. Make a level stitch, thread *below* the needle.
3. Go to the next pleat and make a level stitch, thread *above*.
4. Then go down to the underside (going down exactly where you came out), come up again, and with the thread below the needle, take the fourth stitch to correspond with the second level stitch (Fig. 17).

Dots   Design 2 (page 20)

Another good way to add color. It is made using two pleats.

1. Come up from the underside and catch two pleats together, sewing over and over two or three times.
2. After the last "over," go down to the underside and end off.

Crisscross   Design 8 (page 22)

Quick and easy!

Usually worked in two colors.

1. With one color start on the top dot row, thread *above* the needle, and make three Cable stitches.
2. Go down to the bottom dot row, over to the next pleat, and make three Cable stitches with the thread *below*. Continue across the row.
3. The second color is used to make a second row of Crisscross stitches. This row is fitted into the spaces left by the first row.

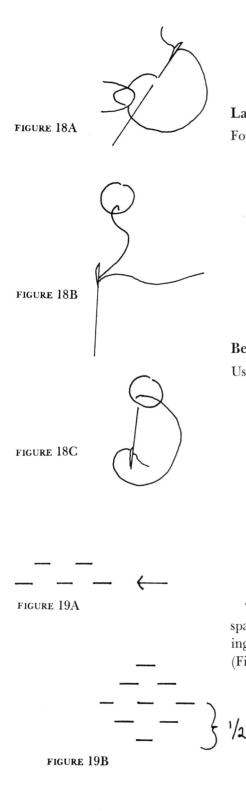

FIGURE 18A

FIGURE 18B

FIGURE 18C

FIGURE 19A

Lazy Daisy   Design 6   (page 20)

For leaves and petals.

1. Come up from underneath. Hold the thread down as in Fig. 18a.
2. Put the needle in right next to where you came out, and up again about ¼″ to ½″ away. Place the needle *over* the thread you are holding down and pull through. This makes a chain (Fig. 18b).
3. Anchor the chain by placing the needle in about ⅛″ to ¼″ away on the *outside* of the loop (Fig. 18c).
4. End off on the underside or go on to make the next Lazy Daisy.

Beehive   Design 9   (page 22)

Use four strands of floss.

1. Come up at the side of a pleat on a dot row. With the thread *below* the needle make five Cables. Put the needle through to the wrong side and come up at the end of the last Cable (Fig. 19a).
2. Turn the piece around and with the thread *below* work five Cables on the side that has the "three look."
3. Go to the wrong side and turn. Starting at the side of one pleat in, with the thread *above* go to the next pleat and make three Cables. Go through to the wrong side. Carry the thread up to make the other half with the thread *below* (Fig. 19b).
4. End off.

The next Beehive should be placed two to two and a half spaces away from the first. Start the second Beehive by making the first stitch on the last pleat of the Beehive just made (Fig. 19c).

FIGURE 19B

½

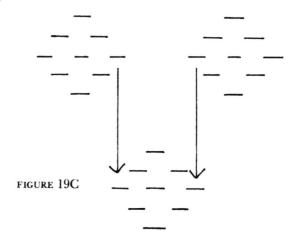

FIGURE 19C

HOW TO CREATE CLEVERLY

These Design Samplers will give you ideas and help with color suggestions.

Put Color in Your Life

Color in smocking is a very personal thing. When we think of babies we think of soft pastels, but a special dress for Christmas could be smocked in bright red and green. Pick up the colors of your evening skirt and a smock blouse to go with it. Whatever colors you choose should be balanced throughout the design. Blue and yellow in the yoke of a dress should be carried out in the sleeves. Use one color, a variety, or shades of the same color.

Copy or Create a Design

It is not as hard as it looks! Central designs are made up of combinations of stitches and rows. Start in the middle and complete the center row. Then add the stitches that go above and below. Work the whole design for about 2 inches to see if you like it and to be sure it is correct.

If you want those baskets centered, this is the way to do it. Fold the pleated material in half to find the center and start there, working out to one side. Now turn it around so it is upside down and work out to the other side.

When the creation is finished, pull out the dot threads. It is time to get rid of the dots. Use a mild soap like Ivory, and soak the piece in warm water. Rinse several times. Don't panic if the dots don't come out right away. It may take several washings.

SAMPLER OF SMOCKING DESIGNS

Designs 1 through 12 will give you ideas for creating beautiful stitch combinations.

Design 1 is easy and is on the toddler yoke dress, page 31. It is also suitable for an apron by working Waves instead of Cables on the bottom. It is made up of Cables, Baby Waves, Baby Diamonds, and Simple Waves.

Design 2 is on the pillow, page 27. It is more involved because the baskets should be centered. Start with a center row of Quarter Diamonds. Large Waves and Cables are added to make the basket. Dots and Lazy Daisies make the leaves and flowers. Quarter Waves and Turret stitches complete the design.

Design 3 Most of this design is on the caftan, page 37. There is a center row of Quarter Diamonds with Large Waves and Quarter Diamonds above and below. Flowerettes are placed in every other Diamond. The top and bottom borders are made up of a Cable row and Baby Diamonds.

Design 4 Ronnie's Rompers, page 30. Make a row of Baby Diamonds. Add a Baby Diamond and Simple Wave above. Skip a space and repeat the same stitches but going below. The two sections are joined with Bars. The top and bottom borders are made up of Cable, Links, and the Wheat stitch using Cables.

Design 5 The center is three rows of Quarter Diamonds joined by Bars. Above and below are Quarter Waves with Large Waves on top. Above are Large Waves with nine Cables across. The very top has two rows of Cables. On the bottom are triple Simple Waves.

Design 6 is a series of separate designs suitable for sleeves or small areas. The first is a variation of Baby Waves and Cables. The second consists of flowers and leaves of Lazy Daisy, Flowerettes, and Bars. The tree is a Bar with Cables and Outline. The third contains houses made with Bars and Large Waves, chimneys made of Simple Waves going up and down using two pleats, and doors, which are Baby Waves.

20

Sampler III   See inside front cover.

Design 7 is another basket made of a variation of Links. It's not as hard as it looks! Start in the center making three Cables. Go up taking in three pleats and make five Cables across the top. Then go down, making three Cables. Continue across the row. Repeat to make the bottom of the basket. Fill in with Waves. The borders are Outlines, Cables, and Turret, and the top half consists of Cable Diamonds.

Design 8 The center is made up of five Cables and a large Baby Wave. (A large Baby Wave takes one whole space instead of a half space.) Above and below are five Cables and a regular Baby Wave. The outside borders are Cable rows with Crisscross.

Design 9 Small Beehives are made from Cables placed so that the pleats between fall into Diamonds. Unusual and different, and a challenge! Outline and Cable rows set it off.

Design 10 The center is a series of Cable Diamonds made larger. Above are Cable rows connected with evenly spaced Bars. Each Bar has three Cables added to the bottom. Below the center design is a series of large Half Links. Triple Waves are placed at the lower edge. This is a must for anything that needs the fullness fanned out.

Design 11 The center design is a series of Links bordered by two rows of Outline. The center of the upper border is Quarter Diamonds with Half Links added above and below. Two rows of Cables are on the top and Simple Waves are on the bottom.

Design 12 Tipsy Hearts between Cable rows make the center design. Make two rows of Quarter Waves separated by a space. Connect the rows in the following manner:

a) Top row of waves: Start at the first stitch made working *down* to make the first part of a Quarter Wave.
At the turn pleat, put the needle through to the wrong side and come back up at the beginning of the second wave. Continue across the row carrying your thread along.
b) Bottom row of waves: Start at the first stitch made working up to make the first part of a Quarter Wave.
At the turn pleat put the needle through to the wrong side and come back up at the beginning of the second wave. This completes the joining to make a Tipsy Heart.

Sampler IV   See inside back cover.

Apron with Hemmed Top
Cable.
2 rows of Quarter Diamond connected.
4 rows of Baby Diamond.
Double Large Wave.

3 SMOCKING IS SMASHING

Decisions, decisions—send away for a pattern, adapt a commercial pattern, or don't use any pattern at all!

Rule: Ratio for smocking—for every inch of finished smocking you need 2½ inches of material.

NO PATTERN

The Apron

Don't bite off more than you can chew. Aprons make a good starter! Buy a yard of material and cut two ties, 3″ to 4″ wide, from the bottom. There are two methods for finishing off the top of the apron. One is to hem the edge and then stamp the dots—remember, on the wrong side of the material and with selvages at the sides.

The other is to turn the top edge over 1½″ and press to the wrong side. Then stamp the dots, being sure that at least one row of dots is above the raw edge. (In other words, the first row of picked-up dots anchors the turned-over edge [Figs. 20a and b].)

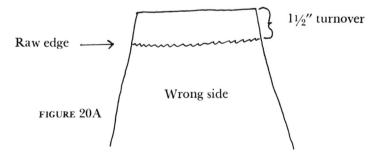

Raw edge ⟶

1½″ turnover

Wrong side

FIGURE 20A

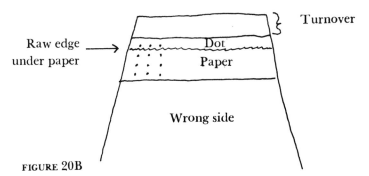

Raw edge under paper →

Turnover

Dot

Paper

Wrong side

FIGURE 20B

Stamp anywhere from five to ten rows of dots. Starting a few dots in from the side, pick up the dots and pull up the pleats. You are now ready to start smocking.

Set the pleats by making the first row a Cable or Outline. From here on have fun practicing the sampler stitches. The last row is usually done in Waves so the fullness fans out and the apron sits smartly and looks attractive. Hem the sides, stitch and attach the ties, and make a deep hem at the lower edge. Don your apron, serve lunch to the ladies—or make it long for a dinner party!

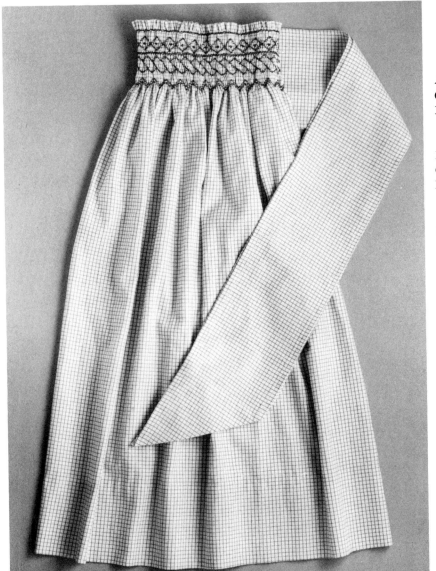

Apron with Turnover Top
Cable.
Large Wave going up and down making a Large Diamond.
Flowerette in the center.
Cable.
Large Wave going up and Large Wave going down with connecting stitches.
Double Large Waves.

Pillow

Turret between 2 Cable rows.   Center design: Quarter Diamonds with extra Large Waves on top.   Cable and Wave on top of extra Large Wave.   Large Waves and Cables on the bottom.   Dots and Lazy Daisy in the center.   Cable.   Turret.

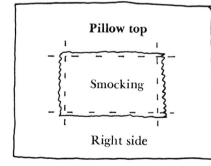

FIGURE 21

The Pillow

A perfect bedroom or baby gift! Cut a piece of material 28″ by 10″. Stamp twelve rows of dots 21″ long with the selvages at the sides. Pick up the dots and start smocking. Trim the excess material to about an inch from the smocking. Center the smocked piece, stretching gently on the pillow top; pin and stitch it down (Fig. 21, Design 2). Frame the smocked section, covering the stitching with strips of material and fancy ribbon. Add a ruffle around the pillow top by placing the raw edges together. With right sides together stitch the pillow top and back around the edges. Leave an opening for turning. Blind-stitch the opening closed.

27

Three-in-one
Cable.
Quarter Diamond with Large
  Wave above and below (the
  Large Wave has a Cable at its
  peak). Bars spaced between the
  Waves.
Double Simple Wave.

Three-In-One: Nightgown, Maternity Dress, or Sundress

The picture above has a front and a back that are smocked alike. Measure the area to be smocked, pulling the measuring tape tightly around your underarms. Multiply by two and a half. This gives you the amount of material needed for smocking. Divide it in half to give you what is needed for the front and the back.

Generally the material comes in 45″ widths. You will need to buy your length for the front and back pieces and enough for the hem, top turnover, and straps.

Cut the front and back pieces to the proper length. Turn the top edge over 1½″ and press to the wrong side.

Stamp the dots, being sure one row of dots is above the raw edge. Stamp seven to ten rows of dots, being sure the dots are placed the same distance from the top edge on both front and back pieces. Smock the *back* first (in case a mistake is made!); then smock the front to correspond. Set the pleats by making the first row a Cable or Outline. The last rows should be Waves to fan out the fullness. Join the front and back sections by sewing the side seams. Add the straps and turn the hem. Now you are ready to hop into bed, waddle over to Granny's, or have fun in the sun!

Be a Good Granny: Baby's First Gown

Cut the pattern out of lightweight material. Begin with the sleeves by making a tiny hem at the wrist edge. Stamp the dots above the hem on the wrong side of the material and on the wrong side of the front pattern piece. Pick up the dots and start smocking. Set the pleats on the first row of the front with a Cable or Outline stitch. The last row should be a Wave to spread out the fullness. Last of all put the gown together. Baby is now ready to be christened!

Baby's First Gown

Cable.

5 Cables with a Baby Wave going up.

5 Cables with a Baby Wave going down.

Flowerette set between the Cable sections.

2 rows of Quarter Wave with connecting stitches forming tipsy hearts.

Cable.

Baby Wave with a double Simple Wave forming true hearts.

Cables on the sleeves.

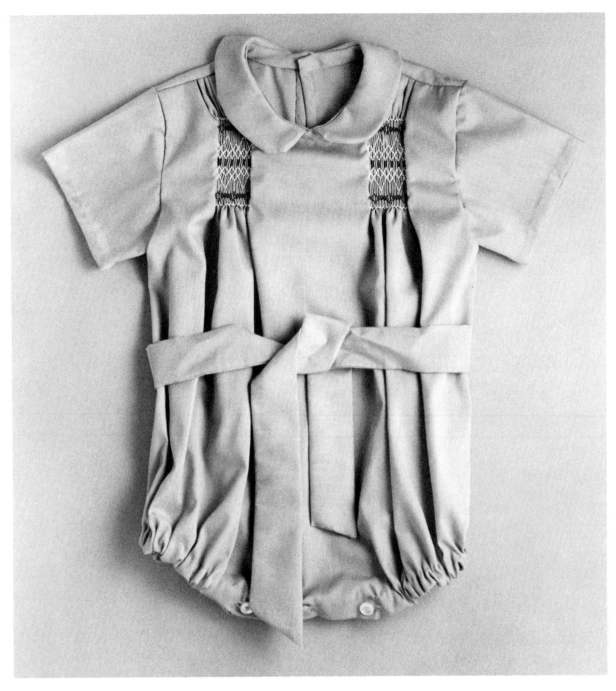

Ronnie's Rompers
Cable.   Cable and Baby Wave going up and Cable and Baby Wave going down.   Center design: Baby
Diamond; Baby Wave and Large Wave above; Baby Diamond; Baby Wave and Large Wave below.
Bars connecting Diamonds.   Cable and Baby Wave going up and Cable and Baby Wave going down.
Cable.

Ronnie's Rompers

Boys are in the act too! An easy shirt can be made from the top
of the romper pattern to mix and match with fancy pants. Design 4.

Little Girl's Yoke Dress
Cable. Baby Diamond. Baby Wave. Center design: Baby Diamond with a Baby Diamond and Simple Wave above and below. Baby Wave. Baby Diamond. Cable. Cables on the sleeves.

Toddler Yoke Dress

This is "The Smocked Dress" every little girl will remember. It has a tiny collar, puff sleeves, and wide hem. It's adorable! Design 1.

COMMERCIAL PATTERNS

**Rule: Ratio for smocking—for every inch of finished smocking you
need 2½ inches of material.**

There are very few commercial patterns available for smocking.
They can, however, be adjusted. Some patterns have no fullness, whereas others have a little or a lot. For the pattern that
has *no* fullness (the front panel in the sundress, photo 9 page 35):

1. Measure the pattern piece *including* the seam allowance
   and multiply by two and a half. This gives the extra
   inches needed for smocking.

2. Subtract the pattern-piece measurement from the extra
   inches. This gives the actual inches you need to add.

EXAMPLE   pattern piece $= 8''$

$8 \times 2\frac{1}{2} = 20$

$\underline{-8}$

12—Number of inches
to be added to
the pattern

If the pattern piece is placed on the fold, divide the number
of inches in half (Fig. 22).

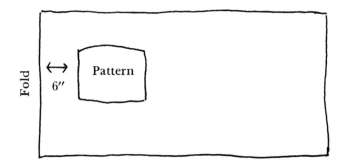

FIGURE 22

For the pattern with *some* fullness (a raglan-sleeve peasant blouse):

1. First measure the pattern piece for the front. *Do not include* the seam allowance. Multiply by two and a half. This gives the extra inches needed for smocking.

2. Subtract the pattern-piece measurement from the extra inches. This gives the actual inches you need to add to the front.

    EXAMPLE   front pattern piece = 12″

    $$12 \times 2\frac{1}{2} = 30$$
    $$-12$$
    18—Number of inches
    to be added to
    the pattern

    If the pattern piece is to be placed on the fold, divide the number of inches in half, as in Fig. 22.

3. Do the same for the back of the blouse. Do not add any inches to the top of the raglan sleeves because they have enough fullness. Generally the lower edges of the sleeves do not need to be changed. They usually measure from 17″ to 20″.

For patterns with a *lot* of fullness (the caftan, page 36) just add a few more inches to the gathered pattern section.

Beauty in the Bedroom: The Nightgown

Most nightgowns have some fullness. If the pattern piece to be smocked is a yoke, it can be made up in two ways. Both methods will need extra fullness added. In the first method add fullness to the yoke and follow the pattern directions. In the second method the yoke and the front are all one piece. Bind the armholes with satin ribbon, with ties at the shoulders. Easy to make and lovely to look at!

Nightgown
Cable.
Cable with Baby Wave.
Quarter Diamond with a Simple Wave on top
  and a Link on the bottom.
Triple Large Waves.

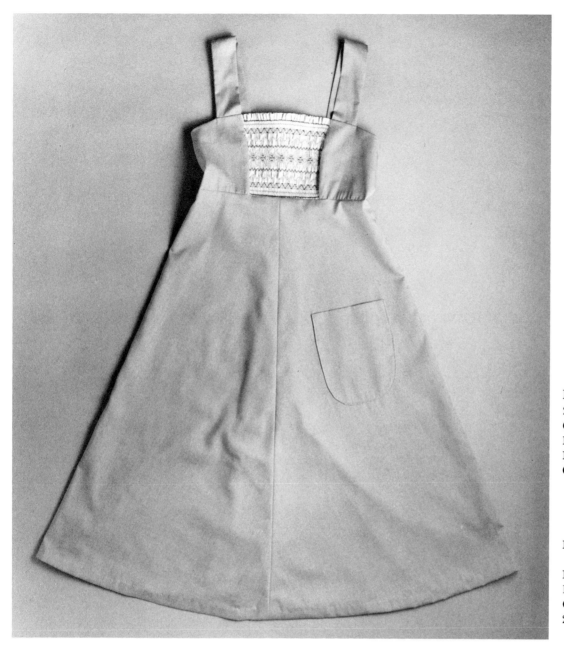

Kit's Sundress
2 rows of Cable.
Crisscross.
Large Wave.
Baby Wave.
Center design: Quarter
    Diamond with Large
    Wave and Quarter
    Wave above and
    below.
Dots placed in the
    Diamond sections.
Baby Wave.
Large Wave.
Crisscross.
2 rows of Cable.

Kit's Sundress

Measure the pattern piece to be smocked including the seam allowance, and multiply by two and a half. This gives you the necessary material needed for smocking. The pattern piece to be smocked will need adjusting because it will have a finished edge at the top instead of a facing. You must add one extra inch to the top of the pattern piece to allow for a turnover, as in Figs. 20a and 20b. Remember this pattern piece is placed on the fold of the material. Press the seam allowance on the top edge and then stamp the dots, following the curve of the pattern, as in Fig. 24a or 24b. Set the first row with a Cable or Outline; next plan a central design. The last row or rows should also be worked in Cable or Outline because the fullness should not be fanned out.

The Caftan

Cable with Baby Wave.
Cable.
Cable with Baby Wave reversed.
Center design: Quarter Diamonds with Quarter Wave
and Large Wave above and below.
Flowerettes in the Quarter Diamonds.
Tipsy hearts.
Triple Large Waves.

The Caftan

This pattern has almost enough fullness in the gathered front to make it suitable for smocking as is. Add a few extra inches by placing the pattern an inch or two away from the fold. Finish the top edge, following the package directions, but remember to add a few inches to the top band.

Fancy Dress Shirt

This is easy to smock but not too easy to put together!

Treat your man to a new drip-dry shirt with French cuffs. Buy a yard of 45″ material that is similar to the shirt.

Stamp thirteen rows of dots with the selvages at the sides. Pick up, tie off, and start smocking. On the shirt front you are smocking across the width of the material, but remember the design will be running lengthwise (Fig. 23)!

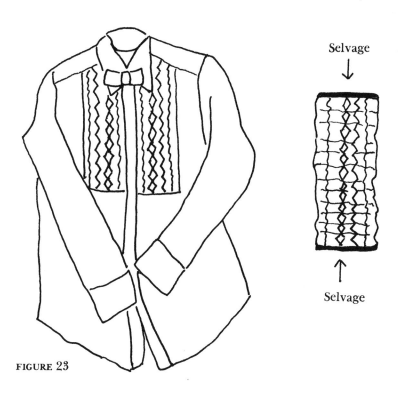

Selvage

↓

↑

Selvage

FIGURE 23

The challenge of inserting the fancy panel: Start with the buttonhole side and open the neck seam to ½" beyond the shoulder. Open up the shoulder seam about 3 inches. Open the inside front flap seam about 13½" down from the top buttonhole.

Cut a hole out of the shirt at about 13" down from the top buttonhole. The width of the hole should be ⅝" less than the width of the smocked panel. This will leave enough material to turn under so it can be joined to the smocked section.

Starting at the bottom, insert the panel under the front flap, remembering the pleats are running horizontally. First stitch the bottom seam. *Stretch* the panel up the front of the shirt and insert and pin it into the shoulder and neck seam. Pin and stitch the side seams, gently stretching. Top-stitch all the edges.

The second side is a little different. Remove the buttons except for the top one. Open the neck seam to ½" beyond the shoulder, and the shoulder seam about 3 inches.

The front flap must be reversed by opening the seam on the underside. (This is later folded over to the front and covers the smocked edge.) Cut a hole out of the shirt at about 13" down from the top button and ⅝" less than the width of the smocked panel.

Stitch the bottom seam. Stretch and pin the panel up the front of the shirt, laying it on top of the opened flap and using the old stitching line as a guide. Bring the flap up and over the smocked edge, pinning in place.

Pin and insert the top edge into the neck and shoulder seams. Stitch the other side seam. Top-stitch all the edges.

Buttons can be sewn back on, or you can make buttonholes and use dress-shirt studs.

A sensational smocked shirt can be made for ladies, using this same method.

If you are tearing your hair out with these directions, call a dressmaker!

Fancy Dress Shirt
2 rows of Cable. Baby Wave. Baby Diamond. Baby Wave. 2 rows
of Cable. Quarter Diamond. 2 rows of Cable. Baby Wave. Baby
Diamond. Baby Wave. 2 rows of Cable.

Peasant Blouse—Back Opening
3 rows of Cable.
9 Cables and Large Wave.
Small Diamonds placed above the Large Wave.
2 Cable rows connected with Bars.
Quarter Diamond with Flowerettes.
Double extra Large Wave.
Sleeves: 3 rows of Cable.
Quarter Diamonds with extra Quarter Diamond above and below.

CIRCULAR PATTERNS

Circular smocking is more involved because you sew the dress or blouse together before you start the smocking. Use sew-on dots or stamp-on dots.

The Peasant Blouse

This is a mail-order pattern (opposite).

Cut the blouse out and make a tiny hem at the wrist edge of the sleeves. Stamp the dots on the wrong side of the sleeves about an inch above the hem. Stamp the dots on the front and back sections and on the top of the sleeves by laying each pattern piece flat and pinning the dot paper across the top. Slit or cut away the paper, as in Fig 24a or 24b. This will allow the paper to follow the curve of the pattern. Be sure the first row of dots is the same distance from the top edge on each piece. (They are usually placed a "seam allowance" away.) Don't hurry

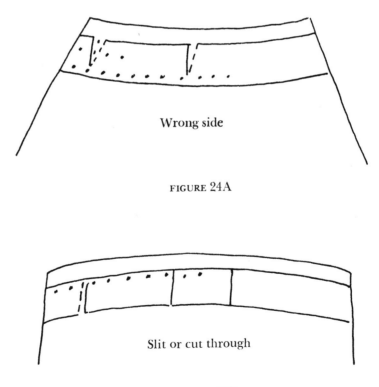

Wrong side

FIGURE 24A

Slit or cut through

FIGURE 24B

this process! After transferring the dots, fill in the empty spaces if necessary with pencil dots. Mark a pencil line down the center back for the placket. This is cut *after* the smocking is finished.

The sleeve wrists may be smocked before the sleeves are joined to the front and back pieces, or the sleeves may be joined and then smocked. Join all the raglan seams, sewing from the neck edge down. Starting at the center back, pick up the dots with one long thread, opening the seams as you sew. Several rounds a day will speed you on your way! Pull up the pleats, making the top rows tighter than the bottom rows. Smock the sleeve wrists, making Cable or Outline on the first and last rows. Set the pleats on the blouse neck with Cable or Outline stitches on the first row. Make Waves at the lower edge to fan out the fullness over the shoulders. Pull out the dot threads when you are finished with the smocking.

Make French seams on the sleeves and blouse side seams only. Starting at the wrist edge, sew one continuous seam. Hem the lower edge of the blouse.

Cut the back opening down about 4″ to 5″ for the placket. With right sides together stitch a bias strip down one side of the opening and up the other. Turn it in and blind-stitch down. Now turn the right side under again and blind-stitch as far down as the smocking. This makes one side lie over the other. A stitch may be taken at the bottom of the placket.

For the neck edge, put the right sides together and stitch a bias strip around the top. Trim the raw edges and turn the bias strip in and blind-stitch down. Sew small buttons on one side of the placket and work loops on the other.

If you are using the sew-on dots, sew the blouse together first. Pin on the dot paper, slitting it as in Fig. 24a or 24b to allow the paper to follow the curve of the blouse. Pick up the dots by sewing through the paper, using one continuous thread for each row. Tear off the paper, pull up the pleats, and begin smocking.

Low-Neck Peasant Blouse

This is easier than the regular peasant blouse because it has a turnover top like the apron or nightie and no placket is needed.

Cut the blouse out, labeling the front and back sections. *Press* the top edge over 1 inch on each pattern piece to make the turnover. Stamp the dots so that the first row is caught in the turnover. Be sure this first row of dots is the same distance

Low-Neck Peasant Blouse—Turnover Top
Baby Wave between 2 Cable rows.
Center design: Large Baby Diamond (made between 2 dot rows) with
   3 Cables at the top and bottom of the Diamond.
Baby Wave with 3 Cables above and below.
Double Large Waves.
Sleeves: Baby Wave between 2 Cable rows.
Baby Wave.
Baby Wave between 2 Cable rows.

from the top edge on all the pieces. Curve the dot paper, as in Fig. 24a or 24b, across the front and back pieces (the sleeves do not have a curve). After transferring the dots, fill in the empty spaces if necessary with pencil dots. Join all the raglan-sleeve seams, sewing from the neck edge down. Mark the center back with a basting thread. This is where you will start picking up the dots and begin the smocking. Remember to have the smocking go all the way around in a complete circle, ending off where you started.

Pull out the dot threads and make French seams on the sleeves and blouse sides. Starting at the wrist edge, sew one continuous seam. Hem the lower edge of the blouse and it is finished!

Little Girls' Round-Neck Dress   Mail order

Cut the dress out, following the directions. Stamp the dots, being sure the first row is the same distance from the top edge on all the pieces.

Pick up the dots and pull up the pleats.

Work several rows of Cable or Outline on the lower edge of the sleeves. Set the pleats on the round neck with Cable or Outline on the first row. Finish with Waves at the lower edge to fan out the fullness.

Pattie is now set for the party!

Little Girls' Round-Neck Dress on Dark Printed Material
Commercial pattern

This pattern will have some fullness but needs more. Add a few extra inches to the front by placing the pattern an inch or two away from the fold. Add extra inches to the back.

Sew the top of the dress together and hem the lower edge of the sleeves. This dress is made of dark printed material, so sew-on dots are used. Pin on the dots, slitting the paper or taking tucks to allow the dot paper to follow the curve of the dress. Pick up the dots, rip off the paper, and pull up the pleats.

Smock the first rows with Cable or Outline. Finish the last rows with Waves to allow the fullness to fan out. Finish sewing the dress seams and the back opening.

Perfect for playschool!

Little Girl's Round-Neck Dress (Mail-order)
Cable.
Cable.
5 Cables with a Baby Wave going up.
5 Cables with a Baby Wave going down.
Combination of Baby Diamond and Simple Wave.
5 Cables with a Baby Wave going up.
5 Cables with a Baby Wave going down.
2 rows of Simple Wave.
Cables on the sleeves.

Dark Printed Little Girl's Round-Neck Dress
Cable.
Cable.
4 rows of Quarter Diamond.
2 rows of Baby Wave.

Becky's Pinafore
Little Vogue pattern #1752.

Apron with Waistband
Cable.
3 rows of Baby Diamond.
Large Wave.
Cable.
Large Link.

FINISHING AND HELPFUL HINTS

Outline stitch worked on the underside of the smocking will prevent too much stretching. It is useful on aprons that do not have a waistband, on little girls' dresses with short, puffed sleeves, and at the wrists of the baby nightgown or dress. It should be worked in the color of the material.

It is also useful when there are "open spaces" in the smocking pattern because it keeps the pleats in place.

Ripping: If a stitch is misplaced, use the eye of the needle to remove it. Don't rip out a lot of stitches. It is better to end off and begin with a new thread because the thread gets worn.

It is not necessary to face smocking since that will restrict the elasticity.

When sewing patterns together, stretch the smocking to fit the piece (as in the fancy dress shirt).

French seams should be made only where the seams may show, as on the lower edge of sleeves.
1. Place *wrong* sides together and pin, making ⅛″ seams. Start at the cuff edge and stitch up the arm seams and down the side seams. (Open the raglan-sleeve seams.)
2. Turn inside out and with right sides together, seam again—this time right next to the smocking.

It is better not to make French seams on smocked yokes like the peasant blouse or the round-neck little girl's dresses because the pleats would be too bulky to smock over.

All threads get tangled. It helps to hold your work up and let the thread dangle down. This applies to regular sewing thread and embroidery thread.

4 TIME SAVERS

Pattern Sources

You can buy commercial patterns and materials at sewing centers.

Mail-order patterns and smocking supplies can be obtained from

Grace L. Knott
Smocking Supplies
86 Larkfield Drive
Don Mills, Ontario
Canada M3B 2HI

Little Elegance, Inc. (for teachers)
Box 14567
Richmond, Virginia 23221

Kiddie Korrall
1011 Sycamore Square
Midlothian, Virginia 23113

COMMERCIAL PATTERNS

Kit's Sundress	Simplicity #8436
Caftan	Simplicity #5478
Little Girl's Round-Neck Dress	Simplicity #7197
Nightgown	Simplicity #7962
Becky's Pinafore	Little Vogue #1752

MAIL-ORDER PATTERNS
Peasant Blouse
Baby's First Gown
Ronnie's Rompers
Toddler Yoke Dress
Little Girls' Round-Neck Dress

NO PATTERN
Fancy Dress Shirt
Aprons
Three-in-One
Pillow

INDEX OF PROJECTS

INDEX OF STITCHES